The National Poetry Series was established in 1978 to ensure the publication of five collections of poetry annually through five participating publishers. The Series is funded annually by Amazon Literary Partnership, Barnes and Noble, Betsy Community Fund, the Gettinger Family Foundation, Bruce Gibney, HarperCollins Publishers, Stephen King, Lannan Foundation, Newman's Own Foundation, News Corp, Anna and Olafur Olafsson, the O. R. Foundation, the PG Family Foundation, the Poetry Foundation, Laura and Robert Sillerman, Amy R. Tan and Louis De Mattei, Elise and Steven Trulaske, and the National Poetry Series Board of Directors.

2016 COMPETITION WINNERS

I Know Your Kind
by William Brewer of Brooklyn, NY
Chosen by Ada Limón for Milkweed Editions

For Want of Water
by Sasha Pimentel of El Paso, TX
Chosen by Gregory Pardlo for Beacon Press

Civil Twilight
by Jeffrey Schultz of Los Angeles, CA
Chosen by David St. John for Ecco

MADNESS
by Sam Sax of Austin, TX
Chosen by Terrance Hayes for Penguin Books

Thaw
by Chelsea Dingman of Tampa, FL
Chosen by Allison Joseph for University of Georgia Press

I KNOW

YOUR

KIND

I KNOW

YOUR

KIND

POEMS

WILLIAM

BREWER

MILKWEED EDITIONS

Published 2017 by Milkweed Editions
Printed in the United States of America
Cover design by Mary Austin Speaker
Author photo by Kai Carlson-Wee
17 18 19 20 21 5 4 3 2 1
First Edition

Milkweed Editions, an independent nonprofit publisher, gratefully acknowledges sustaining support from the Jerome Foundation; the Lindquist & Vennum Foundation; the McKnight Foundation; the National Endowment for the Arts; the Target Foundation; and other generous contributions from foundations, corporations, and individuals. Also, this activity is made possible by the voters of Minnesota through a Minnesota State Arts Board Operating Support grant, thanks to a legislative appropriation from the arts and cultural heritage fund, and a grant from the Wells Fargo Foundation. For a full listing of Milkweed Editions supporters, please visit milkweed.org.

Library of Congress Cataloging-in-Publication Data

Names: Brewer, William, 1989- author.
Title: I know your kind : poems / William Brewer.
Description: First edition. | Minneapolis, Minnesota : Milkweed Editions,
2017. | Includes bibliographical references.
Identifiers: LCCN 2016059859 | ISBN 9781571314956 (pbk. : alk. paper)
Classification: LCC PS3602.R4816 A6 2017 | DDC 811/.6--dc23
LC record available at https://lccn.loc.gov/2016059859

For my parents

CONTENTS

I know your kind, he said. What's wrong with you is wrong
all the way through you.

— CORMAC MCCARTHY

Oxyana (*n*) : A nickname given to the town of Oceana, West Virginia, after becoming a capital of OxyContin abuse. Following a successful crackdown on prescription painkillers, heroin has now flooded the state. West Virginia has the highest fatal overdose rate in America, nearly three times the national average.

I KNOW

YOUR

KIND

OXYANA, WEST VIRGINIA

None of it was ever ours: the Alleghenies,
   the fog-strangled mornings of March,
cicadas fucking to death on the sidewalks,

the pink heads of rhododendrons
   lopped off by the wind.
We wrestled earth with alchemy,

turned creek beds into wineglasses
   the Roosevelts used at state dinners,
fueled fires hot as the sun's dreams.

And there was light: a mile deep
   in the underworld mines,
beaming from our foreheads

like wings through dust.
   Not even the days we called beautiful.
Autumn weekends when DC drove in

to take pictures. Women in silk dresses
   picking our apples, posing,
holding our bushel baskets

with a tenderness we've never known.
   Snow days, belly-crawling
onto the frozen lake

to hear the ice recite the *Iliad*.

  Not Hog Hill where Massey Energy
dumped cinder, the gray waste

between breaths, poisoned trees
    black like charred bones,
where we burned cars while girls

wrote our death dates on our palms
    with their tongues—even now,
rain choking the throats of smokestacks,

the river a vein of rust and trash.

  Have you ever seen so many cold faces
slapped in the afternoon?

So many voices screaming—*Wake up*.
    This is beyond desire.
This is looking through a hole

in the wall around heaven.

  How do you forget that—
a world without ruin,

a world that can't be taken?

  Where once was faith,
there are sirens: red lights spinning

door to door, a record twenty-four
   in one day, all the bodies
at the morgue filled with light.

Who can stand another night
   stealing fistfuls of pills
from our cancer-sick neighbors?

Of the railcars crying,
   the timber trucks hauling away
the history of a million birds?

Pitiful? Maybe. But oblivion is all we have.
   And if we want to chop it down
or dig it up or send it screaming

into our hearts—it's only now
   that our survival is an issue.
Pin oaks arm wrestle over the house

as barrel fires spark like stars in the valley.
   Day closes its jaws.
I can hear my brother explaining

how when Jonah woke inside the whale,
   he didn't know where he was.
I'm not saying this ends with a leviathan,

[handwritten annotation: Pink oaks grow in me]

but I'm not saying it doesn't.

    Here it comes, rising through the floor,
the voice that tells me I'm tired

of the world, that pulls me down
    to its pale kingdom. Should
someone find me, they'll scream

stay with me as they fish
    my tongue from my throat.
Should I wake, they'll ask me

if I can tell them where I am.

ICARUS IN OXYANA

Talk to yourself. Console.
Invoke an image of progress,
failed. Two Vs of geese colliding.
An X, exploding. Pretend
not to worry about your father,
or that he no longer worries for you. Something
about angels, levitation, waking up
with a belt around your arm,
some blood. Tell yourself to listen,
something about your mother,
how she's the best part of you.
A memory of childhood
equated to a bomb. It worries you.
Which worries you. Think again
about the geese. You have migrated through today
through sleep. Someone on the porch
who's lost both his arms
chain-smokes. Something about angels.
Or geese. Or wings. He warns you
about flying too high. Then helps.
Something about chances, not knowing
it was your second till your third
never shows. Summer air. People
blowing up things and celebrating.
Something about pain
as a private choir moving through you.
A movement. A movement. A movement

helps you up. To the porch. To the armless full
of smoke. Where do you want to go?
Nowhere? We have just enough
to get there. And then some.
And then, something. The geese
piercing the sky. They rise, and then, they rise.

HALFWAY HOUSE DIARY

Somewhere at the bottom of the world a whale sings to itself,
running through its temple of otherlight and salt.

I have decided water has a god and its name is gravity.
When it's my turn to fix the gutters, I call myself
Master of the Aqueducts.

When on some mornings, as with this one,
I wake to my roommate bent over my bed,
wrapped in his sheets, whispering,
You're only half-here,
I pretend it doesn't wreck me,
that I don't wonder all day where the other half went.

In the sun's mouth, where for years I pissed heaven?
In the arithmetic of things I was never able to say?

What's the point?
What's lost isn't dead until it's found.

The river ice is breaking up,
smokewhite glass washing over the voiceless stones,
and I can't help but take it personally.

Some nights, a whale song.
I'm halfway here and it's almost too much.

CLEAN DAYS IN OXYANA

You ask what facts I remember from the last five years,
but facts have nothing to do with memory.
When I do think back, I always see the five
buck heads over Crockett's bar, their racks
like the hands of saints upturned and open
to receive the next havoc—how calm
they're made to look after terror, fur still
as infants' sleep. I always thought
one of them must have wanted it, if only
a little, the end—an orange star blooming
between the elms, sound too slow to hear,
unsurprised at the wound's speed,
its determination, like gravity—and the buck running
with the others, not from, but toward, or
into something I have almost seen. It couldn't,
wouldn't have looked away, as it can't now,
its eyes the key to its lifelikeness, what you see
as black glass, I see as the absence of flesh
begetting the absence of light.

[handwritten marginal note, partially legible:] eyes are closer to flesh than they are to glass

FOR KC AFTER LOSING HIS BROTHER

after Eduardo C. Corral

Before the rain the grass

stands straight like an ancient army.

Maybe a cat guts a rat

on the porch.

Listen.

The leaves turn themselves over to be beaten.

A split tree trunk

could be an escape

from the prison of growth

but a broken bone is never

the source of light we think it is.

Listen.

The valley sounds like it's incinerating.

Hay bales

the silent heads of giants.

Choose.

The facts or the memory?

A sheet of rain

cuts over the hill.

A sheet of rain

cuts over the hill

like a knife across a lamb's throat.

9

OXY 40

Think of the mason jar
we use to kill yellow jackets,
the way it's sealed upside down
over the nest's grassy mouth,
how it thrums and pings with desperation,
hundreds throwing themselves
against the light, little empire
with the luster of gold tiles
stripped from an ancient mosaic
of the sun, the incandescence
of a ghost light burning lonely
in the Theater of All
That Could Have Been,
which has been shuttered
to wait out the long winter
descending on your will.

DOG DAYS

In heat this strong I'm not convinced it's not yesterday.
Heat so strong even lying feels like heavy labor.
So when a girl fell off her bike and was crying
in the street, I told her she's living the good life.
When Nate's girlfriend asked me how we met

I said *he shoved his hands down my pants*
and she slapped me before I could say
to stuff them full of ice, to shock my lungs
back into action, to save me. Bars, pool halls,
neighbors turn me away, but not churches,

even though they know I'm only there for the AC.
They're like giant refrigerators full of questions.
Cooling in a pew, I thought: What if god is a fishhook
and euphoria's nothing but a worm lying on his behalf?
No more lying. Now, every time

someone tells me their favorite word is *petrichor*,
I'll say what I've always wanted to: Get over it.
It's not the word you love, it's the smell
of something getting what it desires. The question
most often missed on the West Virginia State driving exam:

"What type of rain makes roadways the most slick?"
It's not a downpour, or a storm that lasts for days—
it's the first rain to break a dry spell. Meaning, if most people

can't conceive of the earth wanting something so badly
that it'll throw away life once it gets it,

how can I expect them to believe in my suffering?

VOICES AS OF LIONS COMING DOWN

—Still brutes? Yes. —Still fools? We?
Of course. Deep January
heavy and forever, way down on us
it sits. Ice-heavy, our needles,
our canopy, sapped. We watched it: the lake

eat the light. All of it. Why
we ask; but nothing. Scraped faces
off the birds, they eat no fish. They
gods of the lake: fish. Under the ice
the gods swim slow, we say.

But I don't believe it. They dead,
and so's the light. And snow,
so many terribles falling. But snow
a comet's tail, maybe, in our hair?
And maybe then where the light

is going? —No. A fault then? —Reckon.
Reckon we involved? —Yes.
And violently? —Violently.

TO THE ADDICT WHO MUGGED ME

Dear Mr. So-and-So with my blood on his clothes,
the Internet says a dollop of my spit
will take the stain right out.

I'm generous like that—I give myself away
to erase any sign that I was here.
What's more brutal:

A never-ending dial tone
chewing the receptors in your brain,
or waking up in an alley with a busted face,

teeth red and penny-sweet, the rain
coming down clear as gin?
Wherever you are

with your stamp bag of winter,
your entire universe boiling
in the breast of a spoon,

floating in a hole in the air
in the middle of a room,
I wish I felt it in me to wish you well.

When goodwill tells me to be tender,
I have a trick: what I'm incapable of feeling,
I imagine as a place—

this throbbing in my brain
is now the sound of your rowing toward
what I pray is, if not home, then mercy.

EARLY OXYANA: AN ANECDOTE

We were so hungry; Tom's hand
on the table looked like warm bread.
I crushed it with a hammer

then walked him to the ER to score pills.
Why'd you keep hitting, he asked.
I don't know. And I didn't. The nurse

asked what happened. Tails, I said.
Excuse me? He called tails, I said.
But it was heads. It's always heads.

DAEDALUS IN OXYANA

Was an emperor of element within the mountain's hull,
chewing out the corridors of coal,

crafting my labyrinth as demanded.
My art: getting lost in the dark.

Now I practice craving;
it's the only maze I haven't built myself and can't dismantle.

I gave my body to the mountain whole.
For my body, the clinic gave out petals inked with curses.

Refill, refill, refill, until they stopped.
Then I fixed on scraping out my veins,

a trembling maze, a skein of blue.
Am lost in them like a bull

that's wandered into endless, frozen acres.
Times my simple son will shake me to,

syringe still hanging like a feather from my arm.
What are you always doing, he asks.

Flying, I say. Show me how, he begs.
And finally, I do. You'd think

the sun had gotten lost inside his head,
the way he smiled.

WE BURN THE BULL

Already flies scratch cursive in the air

Not ten hours dead and like a sun it earns some gravity

Not two months back from Iraq he's swinging the gas can

like a tambourine

Three weeks back I learned the doors of my heart

leak blood but not what that means for tomorrow

my time and strange this sight's what makes me dizzy

I am thinking of the colors fat makes smoke

the coming fire I am thinking

does a disease this mad burn some other shade

Hide frayed and foam clouding out its jaws

in wind like the morning

edge of ocean the sky's color an old blade

and low you don't dare touch else it ruptures

something open if not in you then everywhere

This beast so mad sick it isn't fit for scavengers

to pick-polish bones into broken

furniture its tongue some surrender flag

He points at the bovine's iris hued mercury and blank

I almost wouldn't mind my room that color

We douse the corpse and toss on a torch

like earliest man bewitched by heat's coil

and swell like it's swallowing day's end

and boiling bronze to the surface of hedgerows and bluff

our two shadows leak over as tall and starving pilgrims

You stand there long enough you think you could be cured of something

What was it like

Like the first time you pinch a chicken's neck and spin its world away

It makes you feel like nothing then

No not its world your world goes

It makes you feel like nothing then

If only

NALOXONE

Do you hear that? All the things
I meant to do are burnt spoons

hanging from the porch like chimes.
Do you have some wind? Just a hit

and was the grass always this vocal?
A hit and the blades start sharpening

in the sun. I wear a belt
because my pants don't fit.

My pants don't fit because I wear
the belt. I can tell you how it tastes.

Tannin. Heaven. Is it May already?
As onetime owner of my own

private spring, I can say
it's overrated. Remember? Someone

found me in a coffee shop bathroom
after I'd overdone it

and carried me like a feed sack
to the curb. As they brought me back,

they said, the poppies on my arms
bruised red petals.

They said, *He's your savior.*
But let's not get carried away.

Let's stop comparing everything
to wings. Have you ever even felt

like you're going to not die
forever? It's terrifying.

LEAVING THE PAIN CLINIC

Always this warm moment when I forget which part of me
I blamed. Never mind the pills kicking in, their spell
that showers the waiting room, once full of shame,
in a soft rain of sparks that pity sometimes is,
how it mends the past like a welder seams metal,
and isn't that why we're all here, addicts
and arthritics—we close our eyes completely
but the edges only blur—and though the door's the same,
somehow the exit, like the worst wounds, is greater
than the entrance was. I throw it open for all to see
how daylight, so tall, has imagination. It has heart. It loves.

SUNDOWNING

An empty all-white room with drapeless windows
as winter spills its math across the sills

where nothing suffers, that's where
there's nothing left to misremember

or forget. Here, it's cold, no snow,
no birds settled on the cables, our daylight almost done,

almost. Smog from the steam engine
of dementia tints your hair

and from the first car steps your mother,
who blows into a thin long pipe and blooms a molten poppy

the balm of yesteryear then cools to glass,
a crystal goblet outstretched

whose contents you'd determine but you can't
as your synapses scatter

in the late December forest of your mind
like the torches of Swiss villagers

searching the outer woods of Zurich
for a great black panther that escaped the zoo

in 1932, your year of birth.

Here is your torch, but first, let that living

shadow prowl a few more nights

till every morning becomes night.

ORIGIN OF SILENCE

Even now, out here in the solstice-cold
gathering firewood, ice muscling color
from every silo and shingle, the woodpile
trembling like a calendar of spirit,
cattle on the hillsides getting chiseled by gusts,
snuff-stained pastures, snow-woven dirt,
there is a clarity beyond air, shapeless
yet full, but not with bird flocks scattering
like asterisks against the blue, no,
even now, still haunted, still haunting,
is this silence born the day my brother,
ashamed of his relapse, ran out the door
into the summer air sweet with cut grass
and diesel, mowers hacking
like black lungs, as if he could outrun
himself and, like a grasshopper,
shed a thin, amber husk of his suffering.
When I found him that night across town
at the edge of the rec fields, alone
on a picnic bench, still like a monk
holding vigil, I opened the truck door
and he stood, without words, without
looking, and walked toward me,
almost gliding under the floodlights,
bone-bleached in the glare, with four shadows
pointing in four directions like a compass.
No radio heading home. The dash clock

glowing the green of sun at the bottom
of the sea, windows down but the wind
holding its tongue, a silence so entire
I thought all the crickets hanged themselves.
I said that to him, but he didn't hear me,
not with all that noise inside his head.

WITHDRAWAL DREAM AMONGST SPRING ACREAGE

Here, on the last great ottoman
like all ottomans that once were,

once and always baffled in the patch
of watermelons a violet once green,

and before were gold below stirred air
I stir now, as I always have when

a rumor of sleep stampedes through now
and its disappearance, it too a rumor

outstretched and absolute as this ladder
someone will climb down once I'm gone.

APPALACHIA, YOUR GENESIS

Had you a head I'd set this razor by your side
as a gift then sweep

your silver hair into a bowl, a nest
of strings from a drove of unstrung cellos

half-buried in a field, in a round, like the parliament
of death. Had you a head

you'd have a mouth
and moan the song of a cello played by flame.

From its soot, from clay, you'd assemble your sons, their hands
assemble like air above a creek cattails

hem the edge of like a skirt
the hands slide under in the dark of your infinite

storeroom and wander. Barges
spinning on a mud-sick river. No, some canoe

deaf to the wind on a porcelain lake
black-nailed fingers of a child creep across to pick

the last bits of muskrat stew
that oil-slicks the tongue in a Sunday's light.

Come day from underground your faithful rise
like locusts in a hunger so thick the sun

falls, an accident of wealth
they can't acknowledge for fear it will be taken.

Had you a head it'd be clean, be cool
in its state of without the way some frost is known

by its no longer being. Being who can bless
blessed not this land. No one will say it;

I will. You're nothing
but the burnt edge of an unfinished history.

I press your hair inside a chapter, make a seam
some far-off other will discover

as quicksilver
pooled in their hands. Violence is a surface of ripples,

maybe: points of wind-raked grass
in a valley exhaling with an arsonist's guilt.

Had you a head you'd have ears I am your son
I'd say into I'd say something

about the flies, how on the eighth day
I bound my knuckles in a halo of brass

and punched my friend in the face then spat
on his face on the ground

but the wind caught some spit
like flies made of crystal trying to flee from my mouth.

MY SOMNILOQUIST

for R

To impress I brandish speculations concerning all these passing things:
barges and disease and Goodwill
trucks. I try all things;
I achieve what I can. You try to scan the lines

of my face. I lie when you ask me to paint
your portrait when I say I can't paint portraits.
I can't paint your image, it's the image every portrait
mourns. It's the art we still dream once was.

R, I have never named you here. It's coma of the year, 3 AM, you're asleep
but talking all the time to keep yourself awake. We between
two rooms, between a fear you confuse as you undo it

every night. A better morning is the promise you've kept, keep.
In return: wind through the tree of what I mean
sends an apple through the dark to you.

OVERDOSE PSALM

For how long and why I cannot say,
but in the wake of the great spruce falling,
everything—the axe, its weight in my chapped hands,
the skirt of golden trunk shavings,
the tree like an overturned ship—
is so altered by light, so foreign,
I can't believe it's what I was after,
if I was after anything. And to think
I would survive? It can't be, though,
as so often is the case, it is: the column
of light breaking through the black woods
only a reminder of what once resisted it.
I'm beginning to think that resistance
is everything, how it kept what is now
trees leading to a clearing, a forest.
Snow committing its slow occupancy,
filling the column like words, the light
saying in so few of them, like all terrible
truths, something here did not survive.

RESOLUTION

Today is a new year and winter
and there are so many things
I'm ready to think about.

Like that it's morning
and the power plant
is a womb for clouds.

The clouds aren't real
because no matter
how hard I look I see

only clouds in them, not rabbits
or a pirate ship or hands.
The sliding glass door

before me should be cold
if I touch it but it won't be
because I can't feel anything anymore

after flooding my body
too many times
with an army of synthetic soldiers.

I know this isn't
a solution. I now know
so much more. I know

that last night five thousand
blackbirds dropped dead
over an Arkansas suburb

and it wasn't my fault.
I've only ever killed a robin
and I've never been to Arkansas.

This year I won't feel
responsible. Last night
I was out on the deck

watching fireworks chew
through the air, flocks
of green and gold that showered

back to earth. Last night
in Arkansas, nightfeather
was everywhere. Did they fall

at once or scatter? This year
I won't ask questions
like these and I won't be

disappointed when
I've come up with an answer.
I don't need answers.

I can go to the mailbox
and find a tally
of the grams I've shot up

equated to the hours
of daylight I've got left
and be fine, knowing

that it's time to make
some changes. Last night
was the last night

I'm high. I mean it. While everyone
was drinking and ringing in
the New Year, I stood in the yard

and decided that sometimes
you have to tell yourself
you're the first person

to look out over
the silent highway
at the abandoned billboard

lit up by the moon
and think it's selling a new
and honest life.

All you've got to do is take it.
It's simple, even when you know
you're not the first

to stand on a lawn of frozen dark
and scratch his arm
dreaming of the future.

I know there are ways to feel
different than how I do
just before the train pulls in,

or when I walk the halls
while everyone's asleep,
or when I'm asked to hold

the shotgun, or when my brother
won't give me cash
though he's just trying to help

and way back
in the ruins of my mind
I want to make a blackbird

of him. I'm capable of that.
And so are you. I dreamt
disappointment

is like finding a balloon
in a drawer. Once it floats out
you can't fit it back in.

It just hangs there.
I just hang there on a string.
This year I won't be

OK with that. In two days
I'll admit myself
in exchange for putting out

the white fire on my scalp.
A paper cup, a pill,
an IV's plastic needle

dry-humping an old
stab spot. My bones
will announce themselves

by packing up and moving out,
I'll melt into my bedsheets
like I used to melt

into upholstery. They'll say
the hard part's coming.
When you can't

take anything for the pain,
the pain takes you.
I'll wait. I'll be ready,

I'll look out
my picture window
where across the street

they'll be building a bigger,
better ward. Open floors
of steel stacked up

with tarps for walls
that fill like sails,
a galleon on the caustic waters

of the troubled. Blasts
of light from welders
like headless phoenixes

that would burn my eyes
if closer. Two things
brought together

through an arc
of white energy. I like
the sound of that.

But I'll be there to pull myself apart.
It'll start. I'll hear
a blizzard coming

and think maybe someone
should do something about it.
The cold is already here,

filling up the window.
Maybe the window
was a bad idea?

Imagine that, the first window.
All that light bursting in.
No wind. And the world,

finally at a distance.
A thing to be looked at,
not felt.

DETOX PSALM

Only in the slow braid of a dream
can you study want and need, their
patience, their cruelty. Amid the thin
trunks of their campfires' smoke,
I watched the hours shed
their polished armor, clean and
sheathe their blades, water their
stallions, refuse to leave the shore.
Always a shore, overcast, a sun
that offers me to climb inside its mouth,
and therefore cannot be trusted.
You're asking to be taken apart
without the help of time, in the face
of its broken promise to keep
forward. I thought to give myself
to the dogs, but they only gnawed
my thighs. With the waves' jade
coaxing, I heaved my every organ
through my mouth, then cut a mouth,
at last, in my abdomen and prayed
for there to be something more divine
than the body, and still something
more divine than that, for a torrent
of white flies to fly out of me,
anything, make me in the image
of the bullet, I begged, release me
from myself and I will end a life.

WHAT WE CAN REPLACE

—What's the last thing you remember of fear?

Someone threw my head into a wall.
And the dust of my teeth
burst forth, falling
like fake snow on a stage.

Then I was sweeping me up,
and dumping me into a cup
of milk for keeping. You can't
make sense of what you know

was no mistake. If the sound
of falling glass became
a cold light in my head: the pain
when I opened up to speak. Blind,

we are, to the smallest winds
only a naked nerve can feel,
around us all the time,
like the baby hair of weather.

—It was the winds, then?

Not them. It was knowing
there was one less piece of me
to get in their way.

WITHDRAWAL DREAM WITH FEATHER AND KNIFE

I woke one winter morning to find all my pain
as a lone white boulder in the yard
with a brilliant woodpecker, its head
enflamed with red feathers, chiseling
fruitlessly at the bone-colored surface.
I walked over the frosted grass and snow,
glass needles in my soles, to give the bird
a knife. Wind through the iced branches
like a finger kissing a crystal rim.
In its steel-strong beak, the bird
took the knife and stabbed my hand,
and nothing happened. But the day,
although I know not how exactly,
reorganized itself, each grain of snow,
gears in a blurred engine, fell up
to the sky, through me, through
the way things could have been,
and I understood that—much in the way
we misname some snow as *blizzard*
when it's only snowing with such purpose
that we're estranged from its wonder—
that whatever I have ruined
I have done so according to plan.

IN THE NEW WORLD

Wait till you get a load / of the dead grass smelling / like lemons / Wait till you see how thunder / is a pack of dogs / dragging snare drums / down the street / How the air / over the town square / is smudged with the gray alphabet / of pigeons / apologizing / to the statues / and the statues are totally into it / If you tell the sky / to look away / it looks away with care / If you say let's make a myth of our troubles / I'll say let's call an Oxy / a *moon's tooth* / And a needle? / *god's antenna* / And heroin / *Heavenquick* / On Fridays / instead of sitting in my truck / outside your dealer's house / with my tire iron / dreaming / of tuning his head / to the frequency / of the infinite / I like to park on the ridge / and look out over the future / which is nothing / but a parking lot / shimmying in the sun / Where there's change / there's awe / how every house is made of wood / and once a year / carpenter bees eat them / and we wake up astonished / in a heap of golden dust / with nothing left / I can keep any promise / On your birthday / I'll bury a clock / at the bottom of the river / I'll put on the great overcoat / that is your suffering / all of it / buttons made of what / in the old world / we'd call bravery / We'll feel the earth shift a little / We'll lay your suffering over puddles / We'll watch our neighbors / cross the street / with clean feet

WEST VIRGINIA

Fallen kingdom, conquered first by bedlam,
then bedlam's hunger—hush—heavy
in the air between the hills that crash
like waves into each other. What is a hive
without its queen? Thirst can rule, so can want.
A crown of needles, a gown of clouds she parts.
Bees in the streets below, their tongues
like hands reaching to the sky for an offering.
This is what want does, this and the raindrops
becoming pills in their throats, spurring wings,
all that fluttering the hum of a false heaven.
And who, through that, can hear a few wings
folding under the weight of death? It is too late.
Like timber, like anthracite, death is a natural resource.
The colony glows. The colony does its work.

HALFWAY HOUSE DIARY

Late hour when our knees kiss the floorboards
and prayer or thanks or simple breath
fans like prism-light from the cracks
in our heads, is carried on the wind
across the green tongues of the mountain laurel.
Hour when we each, in our own way, feel illuminated
like the names carved on our desks
caressed by fingertips of lamplight.
I could say gone are the hours
when I am careless with the machinery
of regret, when I let my mind crack a little more,
let the cold years of shame and ruin
spin into the black holes I first saw
as the nostrils of the cow
I found dead in the low pasture,
years back, summer of the great rains,
its snout covered with what looked,
from afar, like dried blood
but which I realized, on approach,
were thick ropes of mosquitoes
swarming down its nose.
Every hour is a version of an hour
coming toward us. How the hour when I wondered
into what oblivion did those eyes stare off
as it fought breath for breath
against death by suffocation,
the hour of too much life to handle,

became the hours when I had to ask the same

of Brittany's eyes, of Elliot's,

half-lidded in a sleep that forgets to breathe,

that forgets the body that holds it,

became the hour when I fail to see

the difference. Death by a thousand wings,

black and fat with blood, or a thousand wings

like embers of a pure, bleached flame.

Hour of drowning in rain.

Hour of drowning in the sound of rain.

And the meadow becoming two kingdoms at once.

TO HIS ENABLER

The night you stopped me at the door
and said *You can't come here anymore, not like this,*
I walked through the narrow fields
deep into an ancient time, on the island
of our ancestors, moss-green and green-damp
and mist, down a sea road, into the waves
that stripped me of what you called
the worst version of ourselves,
and once ravaged, I waded from the surf,
and on the dunes found warm deerskins,
an iron helmet, a battle-axe heavy
and terrible as love, the salt air weaving,
faintly, far off, the song that follows
the slaying of kings, when the fallen crown
is passed around the longhouse
and everyone, for a moment, is a conduit
to the gods, is praised for what thrives,
then blamed for the black mouths of agony
and hunger, and cut down; the terns
outside, spinning like arrows without targets,
Mars throwing down its Martian light,
the North Sea clacking—like the skulls
of rams—the longboats we'll one day ride
into a wound in the earth, chasing the song
that our suffering becomes, I get it now.

WITHDRAWAL DREAM ON THE CAPE

It was the end of an era unharmed
the north sky still smelled heavy of slate
before they cauterized the fens the farms
at oyster bars we'd vaunt our weight
we still had flags before the fountain store
quit selling fountains none could afford
to keep their yachts named *Emerald Vermillion*
ghosts named for colors littered the seaboard
the tide came way in each flag became a noose
I used to wash my apples in apple juice

AGAINST ENABLING

You can't come here anymore, not like this. I said that, it's true,
and because of love, turned my brother away to the dark.

The night was as still as a just-snuffed candle, until there came,
as there always comes after such stillness—or how,

after you've done the right thing—*you're doing the right thing,*
I whispered to myself, I confess—helplessness descends—

thunderheads cracking their knuckles. The rain fell straight down.
Between us turning from each other, a greater kind of trust, I told myself.

And later, like someone smashing clocks on the roof, lightning.
We survived the night only to find, as was true of the morning,

we were not who we thought we were. An unexpected chill,
a small relief. Fall had dragged its brush of tangerine across the trees.

PLAYING ALONG

after Kaveh Akbar

O ancient trout, I know you know: never bank on tenderness.
Your armor is inedible and bends the sun, like a memory
of home—the night woven into a net, your gills
raspy as an organ in a burned-down church. I'm over waking up
pretending to be happy about waking up, sweeping the floor, driving
past rundown shopping malls where people get lit
and dissolve. Home, what an idea; to have one is to become
vulnerable. Am I doomed to a future wherein I'll glow
no more than a match? Will I be lost in a dark, dark wood?
Often I have envied the frail geometry of currents.
More often I have fallen from your sliced-open gut onto the bottom
of a boat and flopped around on your behalf; every bathtub
being a boat on the waters of solitude. When they said it's time
to get sober, they really meant it's time to wake
as bait on a hook cast onto the black tongue
of a river, sinking through breathless dark into the currents
sweetened by limestone. The hook is tied to a line that goes up
past the stars—where it ends, I cannot see. When it tugs me,
I twitch like a living thing; I play along, an invitation
to every mouth that is alone and hungry and without words.

ODE TO SUBOXONE

Of rescuing, impermanent but not imperfect.

The birch of me restored from the paste and paper of myself.

Faded, less. Better-blooded. Suspect of easy heavens. A skeleton

respectable enough for you to be my sentinel.

New schedule: nauseated, wake just as my dependency,

expert as a cougar skulking through the backwoods,

silent like a barge through fog, chases off the last of dark

so dawn can creep inside my double-wide of debt.

In TV's pallid glow I punctuate the minutes with much coffee,

many smokes, reorganize my subjects: the names

and nights of those I've seen and how I almost too have died.

First the rapid deaths. Then those after. Brittany was clean,

KC's brother too. Trees still scratching golden leaves outside.

I hear it all. The cutlery ringing my name from the drawer.

At 9 AM I'll say to you: Good gentle strip dissolving on my tongue,

you summon up my shrieking private want, and like turning inside out

a precious jewel, destroy it, for the day; never let me go.

Of course your leaving makes me me again; you go.

Three hours I'll pace my hideaway alone. Then walk

and wait in line for you and, when I'm told, stick out my tongue

and feel my appetite for worship turn to snow.

THE GOOD NEWS

I cannot explain how I have walked
invisible through a human midnight,
how I understood the night sky
as the space between doubt
and its permanent muscle,
how the pills made my body
an underwater prison, and a whale
flew overhead, turning like the hinge
of hours, I cannot explain how after,
I knew the good news, that *home*
is an ancient American word
for theater, that the light that makes
leaf-shadows tremble on the wall
is an invitation, a way of going back
to the kingdom of the living,
I have seen it, and by the gate
our keys still hanging below our names,
each enameled in moonlight,
a wall of them lit up like the sky
of ten thousand apologies.

LETTER IN RESPONSE TO A LETTER FROM MY SON

Nothing new here.   Still pleading with the ambulances
to teach me their alphabet   so I can know whose name they're singing
as they bleed into the shadow-closet   we call evening.

The takeout boxes are piling up.   When I told you as a boy that you were born
in the Year of the Snake,   you asked,
Is everyone born in the year of what they're afraid of?   Year of the Heights.

Year of the Arachnids.   Year of Already Knowing How to Feel
When I Get the Call.   Your birthday is in a week.
August, of course: the month that tears itself apart.

You wrote: *Quit rehab. Searching for the normal.*
Feel like a ring on the coffee table.   For days, in hopes of understanding,
I've covered ours with glasses of water   that sweat like throats filled with rumors.

Table etched with rings: a potter's field.
I find simple objects to do for me   what I can no longer do myself.
The houseplant sits idly by the window.   I press an ice cube to my chest

and it cries.   What in our blood drives this hearse
we call hope?   The angels in the walls said I must go.
Too much tenderness   can kill those who have forgotten it.

The return address read: *the Injured, the Adored,*
so I'll head that way.   Should you come home how you always did—
when the dark makes its largest sound—I planted night-blooming flowers

so there's something to rise and greet you.

RELAPSE PSALM

I first felt the tongue of warmth and glamour
innocently enough—an ER bed,
two stabs of morphine for my snapped shin
bent like an elbow,
a thousand voices screaming from it.
Then they sang like crystal glasses.

After escaping an obedience to desire,
you fear it.
That, too, a kind of obedience.

Past the window's blackness, I must believe
there is a river, going only by the light
trembling on its surface.
I'm getting better at that—
belief—as in,
I believe this red sound
of wolves coming for me
isn't there.

Either I am hunted
or hunting so slowly
I can't tell.
White fur, white teeth,
closer, closer.

I open a book and see that years ago I underlined,
as if to send myself a message,
"we can be quiet now if we want to be."
But what if we can't?
What if I can't?

If you were with me I'd ask if you hear that—
way out in the woods, a phone ringing
in an empty booth?
But you're not.

No one's here and the phone is ringing.

IN THE ROOM OF THE OVERDOSED, AN EMBER

Oblivion is liberating.

Our names pissed into piles of coal ash.

The curtains move but there is nothing to move them.

You are gone. I am sure.

On time a train wails toward Pittsburgh, except you do not hear it.
Never will again.

There will be no procession. No Adventists on their steps, shaking their heads
in compassion and disdain, no flower wreaths to wrap a room in a perfumed lie.

Our years chew a black tunnel through the mountain.

In this moment of finding you, I do not miss you, which is why I remain
in the absence spun by your denouement.

Curled like a toppled gargoyle.

I wish I could settle on which tense you belong to.

As if it would settle things.

Once as boys we found a snakeskin hanging in the barn rafters and wondered.

Tell me, do pieces of us also get caught on our way to heaven.

A torn T-shirt dangling from your ceiling fan like a cuticle.

No neighbors have risen to their labor yet. Are still citizens of the warm sleep.

Go. Trespass again.

We between the tree line and the valley and the distant smokestack's aircraft warning beacon beaming red like a check-engine light against the dashboard of stars.

You are still here. Each second of late-winter dark is a feather stitching the wings of your ghost.

The coal is almost gone, and soon the mountaintops, and fresh water, after which this will be the cellar of how many centuries, locked away?

Snow wrapping the hills like caul fat.

Cattle on the hills, drops of soot.

The sky is blind and open for the snow.

In the doorframe of your gray, suffocated lips, I place one final cigarette, ember like a diode on an unset clock in the dark.

A paralyzed firefly, a faulty flare.

An offering for the world that promises to take you. It must.

Or else this is not a world.

THE MESSENGER OF OXYANA

Ask winter that has finally arrived,
ask the gray waves of the lake,
that slaughterhouse of light, ask

hour folding into hour,
5 AM, snow clouds pinned against the sky
by treetops bare and black with wet,

ask each flake of vapor threshed
onto the water's gnashing slate
and the indifference of my windshield,

the steel coffin of my truck cab,
dead radio, hoarfrost spiderwebbing
my windows, ask

the fast mist of my tongue,
the air that smells like quarters
in my ashtray, the gashes on my palms

like game trails across a field
to perfect dens, ask the honest cold
how to drive now to her home,

knock and sit and decline a tea
and say that I have held a mirror
beneath her brother's nose and watched

its glass go undisturbed by breath,
I have held the still hive of his head,
have placed my lips against the shadow

of his mouth, screamed air into his chest,
watched it rise like an empire then fall
into that one and stupid sleep.

EXPLANATION OF MATTER IN OXYANA

At Crockett's bar, the last
of the old glassblowers,
drunk, his sand-filled lungs
telling time, says I'm wrong
about the laws of the universe.

Fire isn't matter. It's plasma.
It's process—flame and light...

What about that white glow,
both energy and brilliance,
deep in the furnaces
you blew in, I ask.

That, he says, that's *becoming*—

I ask what became of you,
I say your name,
he says we hold only empty names.

I tell him how the night you died
I ran into the yard, shoved
snow in my mouth,
and screamed your name,
the steam braiding out
like when some forged thing
is quenched in a slack tub,

metal hardened, beaten
to its final purpose,
I swear something iron
fell from my tongue ...

He says the heart
(factory of blood) is iron,
names are only ever glass.

TODAY I TOOK YOU TO OUR OXYANA HIGH SCHOOL REUNION

It was held in the gymnasium   which was full of coffins   full of smaller coffins
full of Oxys.   I guess we were underdressed: me in my surf shoes   you
in an urn.   During the cocktail hour   faces I'd forgotten   asked me
what I do.   I listen for the wisdom of the clouds, and you?   They asked me
to recite a piece   so I ran through the halls   screaming rapture
is watching a little girl   with a flock of gold balloons   tied around her wrist
float away   into a hailstorm   but they didn't get it.   I said we build
buildings to house pieces of our past   and they laughed   clinked their glasses.
Someone   with their back turned to the audience   gave a speech:
two-thirds of us are dead   I found the bench under the mulberry   where I first
wrote words like *blue jay*   hoping they would vibrate into other words
into other words   into a song   that would make me a little less afraid
less alone   sat down   wept with my head in my hands.   Reunion means
go tremble   where you first felt   helpless.   I ran down
the rec field   holding you like a football   hoping to disassemble
but remained whole and useless.   No memories left   just the bleacher
we climbed on a spring night   and I said   if you want to quit then quit doing it.
I owe you an apology: in February   I climbed a mountain in Vermont.
I should've brought you with   should've thrown you in fistfuls   into arctic air.
Things were winding down   people stacking chairs   dragging the coffins
onto a flatbed   when a classmate walked up   and pointed at you
in the urn I cradled like an infant   said that motherfucker
stole forty bucks from me.   I offered him a twenty   I said I'm sorry
it's all we have.

ASCENT

When the little night
light in your throat

grows a tongue and asks
to be transformed

into a blue ribbon
of smoke

that will coil from the hole
you've just bored

through your forehead,
out into the morning air,

drifting like a row
of moths, heavy

with the disappointment
born in that moment

when you realize
that the field of you

waking up in copper sun,
is not as useless

as you'd thought
or hoped, tell yourself

the blue ribbon will tie
to a fence post

like a memorial
even the deer will see

as the strip of sky
you've just replaced.

OXYANA, WV: EXIT SONG

We can't go on pretending that the sky is empty,
that the tin-plated clouds haven't hung over us
for seven years, that our constellations
aren't broken bottles glinting in black puddles.
Because as long as the glassworks' windows
are without the twitch of furnace light
raging orange against the morning,
as long as the river docks slump like old fruit
and sink, and the flatbeds sit lacquered
with leaf rot, we can't pretend
half a town will stop rising every hour
through a lifetime's worth of grace.
Know that it feels as cruel as it sounds,
that I forget everything except the one thing
I cannot. That I am sorry that I love
what I am sorry for. Sorry to speak of love
as if you believe it's still shaking like a mouse
in one of the corners of my chest. Know
that the parts of us we think long dead return
when we lose something else for good,
as when I watched my teeth wash down a gutter
like coins into a well, and against everything,
I wished on them. I can't pretend
that waking this afternoon to a dog
crawling out of my track mark toward home
wasn't the final loss, that that isn't
what we call pain: the dogs. Now my name

is the song of the four legs ambling beside you.
Kneel down; run your thumbs like knives
behind its ears. Rest your nose in its fur
that smells, even wet, like burnt grass.
You, who have kept so much, its keeper now.
And know that without the certainty of pain,
the vulture that is fear loses faith, dissolves
into the gray. It must be that we're all so close to this
that we have no word for it. This minute when,
as I can just make out the spirals of rain
kicking off the bridge that arcs
like a rib above the ravine, I hear,
from down in the river, the harmonies
of a hundred currents weaving
through sunken vessels worth dying in—
a claw-foot tub, a pickup truck—and know
I've already started toward where I'm going.
Know the cost of rising through a lifetime's worth of grace
is a life. That in the hour, as the dark lowers its chin
and the rain glazes to ice, as the streetlight
throws down its brittle halo, as I fade
for the last time, that like one of the rare substances
that expands when cold, with every shiver
there is more of me for the rain to fall through.
And I fall away with it, bleeding down the scrub banks
to the river, free at last from our empire of ruin,
back into the cold hours choked with soot
and mineral, flowing a steady course north
like the Nile, only more ancient and afraid.

THERE IS A GOLD LIGHT

Kind of absurd I still wake up thinking you're alive.
It lasts maybe two seconds. A lot's changed since you've gone—
I've been so shocked by beauty my toenails went black.
As a way of bringing people together, I've started stealing

stop signs. Each morning, I put on my best suit, stuff it
full of dried grass, and go walking through the fields.
The crows totally lose their shit and I feel dead
and alive in that blurry way it got for you near the end—

high, not high, nodding off, so bent over
it seemed your spine was made of feathers. People say
I'm performing grief. I say I'm keeping things alive:
tomatoes, peppers, cucumbers, melons. The more still

I stand, the more flies do their fly thing, sewing up
the spaces between seconds. I want to kill them.
I want to pick off their wings and paste them on my eyelids.
When I bat my lashes, I'll levitate a little. I'll buzz.

For lunch I chewed up bread for Grandpa and fed it to him.
It was like putting coins in a busted jukebox.
Strange thing: I watched his eyes, blind as bowls of milk,
trail the curlicue flight path of a cardinal. On the walk

from his house, the barn, rising from the green wheat,
looks like a rogue wave with a hankering to drown.

Tidal force of dove-gray wood, hay-scratch, ribbons
of snakeskin hanging in the rafters. I've come up

to the hayloft to gather tomorrow's courage
and wonder out loud if maybe you were the cardinal,
but there are bigger miracles at hand. It's the evening hour
when the sun, through the cracks in the wall, slides

over the floor like golden doors to something as desperate
and false as prayer. As if my grief were a hall. As if
it were of any use to the dead. How can this not be for you?
I would have done anything.

NOTES

The epigraph comes from Cormac McCarthy's *Blood Meridian: Or the Evening Redness in the West* (New York: Vintage, 1985).

"Voices as of Lions Coming Down": This title comes from Wallace Stevens's poem, "The Sun This March."

Naloxone (brand name Narcan) is an opiate antagonist that can stop an opioid overdose within minutes of being administered.

"The Good News": The phrase "a human midnight" comes from Wallace Stevens's poem "The Souls of Women at Night."

Suboxone is a combination of buprenorphine and naloxone used to treat opiate addiction.

"There Is a Gold Light": This title comes from Donald Justice's poem "There is a gold light in certain old paintings."

ACKNOWLEDGMENTS

My deepest thanks to the editors of the following journals, in which some of these poems—sometimes in different forms—first appeared:

The Adroit Journal: "Resolution"
Bennington Review: "Oxyana, West Virginia," "Relapse Psalm,"
    "Today I Took You to Our Oxyana High School Reunion"
Bodega: "Withdrawal Dream on the Cape"
Boston Review: "My Somniloquist"
Carolina Quarterly: "The Messenger of Oxyana"
Colorado Review: "West Virginia"
Columbia Poetry Review: "Icarus in Oxyana," "Naloxone"
The Common: "Daedalus in Oxyana," "Detox Psalm"
DIAGRAM: "Appalachia, Your Genesis"
Diode: "Against Enabling," "Halfway House Diary," "Oxyana, WV: Exit Song"
Horsethief: "To the Addict Who Mugged Me in Oxyana," "Playing Along,"
    "There Is a Gold Light"
The Journal: "We Burn the Bull"
Kenyon Review Online: "Voices as of Lions Coming Down"
Linebreak: "In the Room of the Overdosed, an Ember"
The Literary Review: "Clean Days in Oxyana"
Muzzle Magazine: "Overdose Psalm"
Narrative: "Dog Days," "Letter in Response to a Letter from My Son"
Nashville Review: "Leaving the Pain Clinic"
Phantom Books: "Ascent," "What We Can Replace"
The Pinch: "For KC after Losing His Brother," "The Good News"
Pleiades: "Halfway House Diary"
Poetry Northwest: "Oxy 40"

A Public Space: "Sundowning"

Quarterly West: "Ode to Suboxone"

Southern Indiana Review: "In the New World"

I am grateful to the editors of *Narrative* for awarding "Dog Days" and "Letter in Response to a Letter from My Son" as part of the 2016 30 Below Contest.

Portions of this book make up the chapbook *Oxyana*, which was selected by Marilyn Nelson for the 2017 Poetry Society of America's 30 and Under Chapbook Fellowship. To both Marilyn Nelson and the Poetry Society of America, I offer my sincerest thanks.

An endless loop track of thanks to Ada Limón for believing in this book.

For their generosity, support, and belief in my work, I offer thanks to the following institutions: Allegheny College, the MFA program at Columbia University, the National Poetry Series, Poets & Writers, the Sewanee Writers' Conference, the Wallace Stegner Fellowship program at Stanford University, and the Vermont Studio Center (especially Laurie Macfee and Ryan Walsh).

I would be nothing without my teachers: Mark Bibbins, Lucie Brock-Broido, Dorothea Lasky, and James Richardson. I am especially indebted to Christopher Bakken, in whose class this all began, for his belief, encouragement, hospitality, and friendship, and Timothy Donnelly for his generosity, patience, guidance, support, and friendship.

So many people helped me make this book, sometimes through nothing more than camaraderie, conversation, and encouragement, especially Malachi Black, Justin Boening, Ash Bowen, Anders and Kai Carson-Wee, Brandon Courtney, Kwame Dawes, Kelly Forsythe, Amber Galeo, Hafizah Geter, John Hennessy,

Peter LaBerge, Brett Fletcher Lauer, Ricardo Maldonado, Maurice Manning, Elizabeth Metzger, Matt Miller, my *Parnassus* family: Herb, Sue, and Ben; Catherine Pond, Richard Quigley, Camille Rankine, Max Ritvo, Laura Romeyn, Sam Ross, Danniel Schoonebeek, Emily Skillings, and my VSC family: Henry, Joe, June, and Stew.

To everyone at Milkweed Editions: You are the dream.

To my parents, the Grogans, and my siblings, thank you for everything.

And to Ryann, for everything else.

Kai Carlson-Wee

WILLIAM BREWER is the author of *Oxyana*, winner of the Poetry Society of America Chapbook Fellowship 30 and Under. His poetry has appeared in publications such as *Boston Review*, *The Nation*, *Kenyon Review Online*, *A Public Space*, and *Narrative*, where he was awarded the 2016 30 Below Prize. Currently a Wallace Stegner Fellow at Stanford University, he was born and raised in West Virginia.

milkweed
editions

Founded as a nonprofit organization in 1980, Milkweed Editions is an independent publisher. Our mission is to identify, nurture and publish transformative literature, and build an engaged community around it.

milkweed.org

Vendetta was designed by John Downer for Emigre in 1999. The typeface stands as an expressive personal homage to the roman punchcutters influenced by Nikolai Jenson's 1470 tract, *De Evangelica Praeparatione, Eusebius,* while incorporating aspects of the Incunabula period of type design with contemporary concerns for optimal digital display.